One Equal Eternity

Poems of Passage

One Equal Eternity

Poems of Passage

Kate Brophy

Death can be a void that carries a swift terror, and like ice to the flesh, freezes to the bone.

Death carries that marker, that aura, that publicity, and we can shudder, and flee and hide until death passes, and close our eyes tight against another void awaiting in the future.

So it is to this lurking menace, the vast and endless darkness that haunts our dreams and lurks around the corners of our frailty and mortality. This chalice of the void is what we might embrace in the poems that follow.

Death is the void of mystery and scariness, humor and longing. The path of dying and death itself are worthy of our attention, our respect and our love. Death and the journey to death are not morbid or depressing, because this final moment is surrounded by surprise, sorrow, struggle, laughter and our very deepest humanity. May we celebrate all its beauty and its attendant mystery alive with right now and eternity. Forever.

The Quiet Journey

I pray for golden wings
to carry me beyond the sun
to hold me safe
across the silver night
to the other side of the moon
where there is no fear
and freedom gives
safe harbor in the
dark nights of life

I pray for quiet journey
into hope
where life and death are one
and in each moment
the curtain rises
on a new and splendid place
where beauty never ends
and joy sings wild songs
to keep eternity alive

The Enemy – My Friend

she called me to come.
I went through the dark bleak hallway
of the city hospital.
I went with cold fear
to greet my first dying, my friend,
whose face I would not see,
a face I knew through many years
full of kindness for all
whom she knew little or well.

I could not look at her
she who loved me and
presented me with the first face
of dying.
I was ashamed.
I was guilty of no sin but fear and that ignorance
that climbs up
out of heavy rule and law
and constructs pretenses and fantasies
and makes masks and
cements them to the heart.

a dangerous day, this dying moment
no place for youth and beauty
and all the circus fun that
thrills and kills a day
the radiance of adventure
that circles time and shuts out
the thoughts of endings.

the room is an ice locker
and my friend is holding out her
hand to me. I cannot take it.
her final days are not acceptable,
I will not allow her to touch me.
she will die. I will not forget. ever.

A Little Poem

no more pointy shoes
flowing silks
and shantungs
no more brilliant prints
with tight bodices
and plunging necklines
silver-lined deep pockets,
trinkets and trips,
excitements of discovery
and plans of conquest,
all moving into the distance.

it is good to awaken
and know that the riff
and the raff of
living in a culture of more and compare
is nearly over
this grand event – living –
lies gentle in the distance,
the land of always beckons,

where only the soft song of a dove
is heard
and on the far deep lined horizon,
a halo of light surrounds the universe.

Shall we Speak of "Old"?

It is thought to be tragic
this growing weak and listless
losing our way and our wits
not finding old comforts
or new desires makes "old"
a frightening place.

"old" means so little time left
"old" halts and falls,
weeps too easily
and forgets its breakfast bread.

"old" is grace, it is quiet
it is a peace that gratifies
and terrifies
"old" is not to be spoken.
It is to be hushed
to be erased.

Where does this fear first live?
Where does it birth its power to resist

the falling of a star
the pull of the earth
that pushes away the sun and the moon?
This fear that puts tears into waning hours
and leads us to resist the pains and sorrows
that invade the flesh
and pour us out like unmerciful libations?

"old" is a grandeur
quiet and hidden
secret and mysterious.
"old" is a landscape
that inhabits our lives
and pleads to be celebrated
so that we, who reach that aged place
may rejoice in its feverish
and seamless hope.

I Believe in Death*

death holds everything, just so
everything.
Its music, its heart
its dance and rhythm
is full of measured beats,
pleasure, sadness
the tension of befores and afters,
the light and dark of life,
the peace and violence of experience
the hope and despair of the daily
importances and trivialities.
Everything converges into one
simple creative moment that halts
the whole show in progress.
Death changes the landscape,
but shifts nothing.
Its life pushes into new places
to bring forth exquisite possibilities
that hold a truth unexamined.

that's the mystery of death
that pins us to our fear
and will not let us see
the extravagance of possibility
that rests in the heart of last breath
and kindly holds the door open
for all the impossible hopes.

*Mary Oliver

Choice

it was Friday
and the call came down.
it was like a voice from out in
the darkest boundaries of space
an echo, really,
it was a clear challenge
"you have cancer
you have cancer, fourth stage"

how can one have
anything so impertinent
and dangerous
announced like a roll call
or a directive from an
authority outside humanity

where does one go
with such a voice
an echo that pours forth
an elegaic fog into
an innocent day?

a call to arms
a girding for battle,
a pause,
and a recognition of foolishness.
Whoever won a war
or even a skirmish
when death seems to be
the only show in town?
Somewhere between
life and death
there is a wide
and endless space
a place that brings
an invitation to come
be with this dire notice
of dying
come and find a new
home to grow up in
and learn to speak
new hellos and goodbyes.

Sister

I have a sister who
has been with me for
seventy-five years.
she has been a doorway to
a wider space, a deeper place –
a fence to guard a heart
a sign post that poses
yields and go aheads
and proceeds with caution.
she is a world of fury and fire
and sublime quiet that
pours out a calming libation
when least expected.

how is it possible
soon
she will be no more
but a lingering imprint
in the passing of a day.

I will not think of it anymore
the waiting is enough, to let
a heart suspend in hope,
and the days of spring to gather
buds and blooms for the soul.

My Sister's Autumn Death

it was time, I guess
whoever knows the moment
when the final darkness
will steal around the corner of a day.

is it a call to eternity?
a whisper heard in the distance
without remorse for its deed
a call that comes when it will
and seizes a soul, giving it a place to hide?

this pale sister of mine
a rambunctious and belligerent
companion, with courage in her eyes
wielding power over a day
until that moment when she uttered these words:

"I cannot walk. I don't know why I cannot
walk."
a simple declaration – a letting go
oh does it mean that time is running out?

the thin edge of night is coming into sight
and the first light of the moon is on the horizon?
She says:
"I live here in this room and
listen to words of comfort about death.
the silence buries me, the quiet and
not knowing bring me to wonder –
and some fear.
I look out the windows and see the
tall thin trees, bending slightly,
and the green leaves moving in the breeze.
it is lovely."

my sister's last words for me
drop into a soul, waiting to receive grief,
and in so brief a moment waking to find
a new place where we might meet,
and resume our debates
and let the words we love
tumble like the soon to come red leaves of
autumn
that will weave a new tapestry
for an unexplored winter.

To Remember

I was alone
the night my husband died
in the hospital
in our new town
I knew no one.

it came time to leave death
and gather my loneliness about me.
I did not cry
I could not cry

I walked out of the hospital
onto the sidewalk
and looked up into the night sky.
there was a half moon and stars
I told them I was alone,
there was no one to speak to
about this death.
fifty-two years we loved
and worked and laughed,

a good man
no tears came

I noticed how clear the
stars shone down on me
the moon looked warm
so I talked out loud
I suppose they heard me
and maybe said a prayer

Death is the Mother of Beauty*

Sweet Roderigo
his curly head resting
on the white pillow
his face,
somber and pure
all of nine years old
waiting for death
to come and steal him away,
he is, now, beyond all hope –
an angel in flight.
like all children,
their arms raised upward
hoping we will see
the hidden beauty of death
that lies in the folds
of each glorious day
and that holds each soul
in quiet embrace,
and brings our children
closer to us than our own breath
*Wallace Stevens

Ole Semple

Ole Semple shod horses
and lived his days with
silver nails between his lips.

a whiny twang
a glum grief
followed him everywhere
but often there was a light
sharp in his eye
a glimmer of humor and
"I know somethin' you don't."

his home was a corral
his comfort holding a hoof
between his legs, rested on a knee.
he flung words into the air
and the horses' ears would quiver
and the head would sometimes give a nod.
"feelin' poorly, yes I am", and often
"close to death as a rattler's belly", a whine that
settled loosely on the dirt.

"Where you from, Semple?"
"east of Wichita, maybe", he always said.
Semple seemed to blow in on a
draft of summer's wind
and no one was going to discover
a story that might be true.

he had a frequent lament
that maybe could have been
put to music.
"My horses stand still as posts
not a moment's trouble.
people now, they come and go.
can make a day not worth a whit,
always messin' where they're not supposed to.
a horse, that's a creature stares down a day
and gives no harm to any man
except who asks for it."

"See this hoof,
it's a tired hoof".
"How you know that?"
"I don't need to know. It's in the feel.
That's what my hands are for.

I feel this hoof
it says to me, 'tired'."
I get the rasp
and I take it down a half inch
lighten the load
now this ole nag will go to
pasture, even work a bit now and then
and never complain to anyone
most of all to me.
That's a job I'll do forever."

so back went the silver nails into his mouth
another hoof on his knee
and a sullen gaze on a crinkled face.

Ole Semple died one day.
where did we put him?
I have no recollection.
Maybe he's up north among the oaks
where it is still,
and only a hawk, frequent and fugitive,
keeps a vigil among the stones.

Harshaw

Harshaw, a ghost town
of the mining past
no more than that

one building still
standing in defiance
of time and weather
and the plain meanness
of withering and disappearance,
the mark of every love,
every dream ever hold close

this pitiful remnant
a brave presence
a reminder that everything
carries a "so what!" notice
in its wood and mortar

across the muddy road
a small cemetery
hemmed and bordered by an iron fence

that small plot of earth
alit with paper flowers
bright bouquets of revelry and sorrow

nothing seems to stay the same
but death
and that makes me mad.

Death of a Poet

"death of a poet" the headline read
credits and applause
he was creative – brilliant, really
and dedicated
a "poet's poet", they said
and the plaudits elevated
his buried hopes.

no more dreams for the poet, merely
words of affection, admiration
and he, nowhere in sight to
hear or read them.

it took him a long time to die,
age fifty-eight. the alcohol swooped
him up in lover's arms
and carried him off
with songs of hatred and disgust.
pleasure gone
each day – kill the pain
he died by his own hand
though neither doctor nor friend

would say so
the drink does that
it turns lovely souls against themselves,
lies to them
tells them terrible fables of
unforgiveness and rebuke
finally, one day, the lies kill them.

some see the truth
but will not speak it
others cry out from their graves
to unravel the truth
that the eye of the storm
is not a peaceful place
but a raging tumult
that hides the knowing.
still, the poet dies
his friends live on
and make up stories
to speak into the dark of night.

Charlotte Has No Wrinkles

Charlotte has no wrinkles
proof that she belongs
to the "beautiful people"
the people of a great and good God.

she has talent galore
look at those "come to life"
paintings of blueberry and antelope
see her swing that arm
and swivel those hips
and send that ball spinning
across the mound
one, two, three strikes you're out sister
the record books shook
with glee, as she filled their pages.

but these gifts
rich and creative
exuberant and life-giving
pale beside the greatest Charlotte gift of all
her presence.

she was there, she was here
she was now.

a shadow, not a pretend one
who went in and out with us.
where the lonely, the distressed gathered,
made from papier mache
there was Charlotte in their midst.
when sadness or panic
swept a heart out of its home
there was a place,
a space, a rest
and a Charlotte smile.

there was no hustle or bustle
no frantic goings and comings.
her feet planted squarely
on the firm earth,
she waited and loved
and wept and laughed.
she was not absent from life
she was often its essence, its soul
its essential force that drives

the slim and flimsy reed of grass
through the dark dry earth.

yes, dear Charlotte received
the infallible gift of life,
its divinity of joyfulness
its remarkable sorrow and
ever present grief.
she wore it all as the loose
garment of acceptance
that covers the troubled earth.
she walked with loneliness and
celebrated the beauty and the
wounds of her humanity and ours.
I am sure that is why Charlotte
has no wrinkles.

Asi Es La Vida

"hello Miss Marian, how are we doin'
this fine day," she chirped
and it was a chirp, like some
treed jay who was without food or mate.
she, being the clever and bright volunteer
who patrolled the nursing home halls
to make sure patients smiled and
knew how blest they were to be in such a
cheery drab slab of sadness and
loss loss loss
more loss than the mind could understand.

Miss Marian smiled and turned her face
toward the window into the pale light
of fading afternoon.
she was not interested in the cheerleader
today or yesterday or for all the
forever tomorrows.

Marian was a fat wide stump of a
brave and disappearing woman.

diabetes claimed her legs
and now her kidneys.
in this boxed room with only a chair,
and a picture of a green tinted stream
wailing through a forest of blue trees
nailed to the wall,
Marian was walking the last mile of life in
midair.
It was not easy.

So little to hold her and bring her to
any place of wonder for this
last event of living.
where was the carnival of joy?
or even a distraction of care?
anything that could part the dull
waters of a day.

the happy face approached the bed
and beamed a smile down on Marian's
round and fleshy face.
"And what do I see here beneath
your pillow, Miss Marian? It's yellow
and blue, a candy bar, I bet." Her voice

an accusing slur.
Marian, all eyes, dreary and blurred
reached up a short stubby fingered hand

and pulled from beneath the white clad pillow
a long wide true-blue and yellow Butterfinger.
a triumphant flag of hope
and the only sign of peace in her eyes.

she shook the candy bar from side to side
and said with glee
"If I die today, it will be with
peanut crunch between my teeth.
This is the one truth I know
or care to know, thank you."

An Extended Leave of Absence

Shirley inhabits dying
like a new dress.
she is comfortable with
the style and familiar lines
distressed at the often awkward fit.

fresh feelings, strange designs
in each day
there are no pleats
but a few wrinkles handled easily.
the colors are muted
and a rare splash of brightness
brings a clap to the hands
how wondrous, joyous
is this farewell parting.
how sometimes dark
as sorrow parts the
night and day
and sometimes shatters all into
falling pieces of unfamiliar fabric.
there are no parties

or frivolous diversions
simply a steady, step by step
due north into the pale light of dawn.
with the nod of her head
a slight smile sewn on the lips
eyes steady
she leans into the moment
and whispers:
"I'll be somewhere never seen soon,
just gone for an extended leave of absence."

I Buried My Dog

I buried my dog in the back yard
I buried her alone
no one else attended the service
of my small blond cocker.
I was enraged because she died
for no good reason –
a mistake, an error in judgment,
a brief carelessness
a door left open, a waiting street
and one laughing pup
was tossed into eternity
only the sky to catch her
and save her
and her keeper's
grieving soul

Not Outside Our Wonder

her rumpled face is pressed
pale against a white pillow.
she rests on her side
without motion,
a quiet, tedious breath
nowhere to go
one eye is slightly opened
and stares into a place long avoided

she is in coma now, they say,
could be like this for days
perhaps, she could be gone in a moment

shall we agree?
but wonder if that half opened eye
is now receiving its true sight
one we, who watch where we step,
know nothing about
is that coma eye pausing

and resting in a space
or frame of life never seen before?
why are we so sure or unsure?

why don't we sit here
with this sweet body so close to death,
perhaps more alive than ever,
beyond our knowing
but not outside our wonder

Breath

death is so familiar
we evade its "notice"
ignore its unadorned presence

life is all about the everyday
moving toward less and less
until one unpretentious moment
welcomes the final exhale

it is such a common letting go
one we have rehearsed
without knowing
millions of times
the breath in
the breath out
and then the breath
is no more

and that's the end
of the familiar
and the beginning
of mystery

I Saw A Star Die

I saw a star die
only once
in a large, bleak classroom
with no windows
and only a screen-filled wall
high above my head.

it was a fiery and fierce dying.
it seems the whole room
filled with vibrant pinks and blues
and golds.
it was a blur of pin-pointed colors
that swept all the rainbows from the sky.

no show in the universe quite
like a star dying, I thought.
it shattered and splattered and
fell into trillions of bits and pieces
of sad and crucial light,
and I wondered then,
as I do now,
is there anything more beautiful than death.

Grandfather Tree

the blue-green forest
awakens to the first light of morning
drops of moisture still perched
ceremoniously on fat iris blades
and wispy aster petals.
aspens, thin and white
shaky green and wet
and in the thick of their quivering,
stand in stone-still homage
to a tree, a grandfather tree
a mighty ponderosa, snapped like a matchstick,
felled, gutted and shredded into thick threads
of sap filled with caramel wood
all mottled with storm and violence.
what swept this beauty to its death
as if it were no more than a
flimsy reed – a lonely moment
burst full of life and then, no more.

flat on the cool green earth
branches splayed with tangled ferns
and matted grass,
a monument to the mercy
or the violence of creation.

Irises

why am I surprised
when the dry cold of winter
begins to disappear.
I look at the cracked soil
in the garden and
there is a thin reed of life
forcing its way
through the clotted earth.
another winter ebbs
and seeds beneath the frozen soil
somehow split open and shoot out
a frail wisp of hopeful spirit.
these forgotten bursts of joy,
believed gone forever,
did not prevent one moment's caress
from an unseen exorcist.
they sprout up, still and yielding free
to receive their message of birth

hidden deep in wrinkled and dry bulbs
and little pips of throwaway.
how bold of them to burst through
our calm morning and
shatter our disbelief.

We Who Are Dying

we who are dying
are not comfortable
in anyone's company
because who wants to keep saying goodbye.
goodbye. what's that but regret
and sadness
and all the last words that never get said.
goodbye. who desires
to linger over coffee and
look into eyes lost in other worlds
or into pain that slices good intentions in half
or eyes that hold on to nothing
or that speak a moment's true words.
why hang out with darkness
and a daily sword piercing a ruined day.
that's what goodbye is,
a disappearing that lingers
in every room
and leaves a funeral in its wake.

nowhere to put all that
unfinished business.
still, each day must be
a goodbye, or a pretend.

Everything Is One Deep Breath

every week I get to receive prayer,
prayer without words,
a deep and penetrating silence
comes to greet me
as I walk through the door
the hospice stretches out
before me, each room
with a quiet and solitary soul
with new heart, new every breath, reaching
toward a point I cannot see
I cannot share.
I am always stunned into a
place within my deepest soul
where the furniture is unfamiliar
but there is a music that is
cadenced to the beat of the heart.
I look on faces that have
a beauty beyond language,
beyond idea or even image
where are they, but someplace
I cannot go and yet yearn to glimpse

just one secret eye catching moment
that is all I desire as I enter
this world of dying.
I want to go down deep inside
that wrinkled and cranky face
and see the wide and generous
life of a tomorrow that is
eagerly awaiting.
I want to step inside that
young brown-skinned, unlined
countenance, eyes closed, a deep sleep
beneath a fitful heartbeat,
somehow I know that beyond this
simple vision called
"what can I observe"
there is a land that would
knock me off my feet
if I could just catch a
swiftly passing eye blinking moment
that would say to me:
there is more to living
than you will ever understand

let go and be careful where you step
everything is love
everything is one deep breath
within an ecstasy always waiting.

The DNA of History

in the distant night
a firelight glows
against the darkening air.
Alert to the stillness
and the practiced
ways of the skies,
a nightlight – anywhere
becomes a resonance of hopefulness that
lightens fears
and calms the panics
of unexpected loss.

Death, unrehearsed comes
unbidden.
Life, in each moment, hesitates
then, in that space of a skipped beat
or, simply, a necessary pause
greets death who has turned up
unannounced to offer its
only promise, "come".

there is a space
between here and now
ever so small
with a faint heartbeat
that signals a continual
life and death convergence
a discovery and disappearance
a conversion
a hope and a wondering.

Death is the DNA of history
it is the requisite
for creation and the question
how beautiful, how simple
is the root and the essence
of the now and the forever
where death spreads
divinity deep into
the universe
and we, still uncertain,
wait to follow, unafraid.

The Land of Sorrow

what is this place called sorrow.
a land all its own
where there are no boundaries.
when we awaken in the morning
and the sunlight calls us forth,
being seems fragile, yet willing
to move into an untraced space.
some days arrive
with angry and fearful drumbeats.
the heart builds patchwork
designs of letting go
and hanging on to every unfinished moment:
restless, useless
gathering scattered
thoughts and plans and dreams
that never received full attention.

did we waste time
not doting on friends
brothers and sisters
husbands and wives

all who passed our way but once?
how long is the list
how deep is the sorrow
that is marked with goodbyes
or blank places where
no events or words took place.

What do we do with all
this melancholy longing
for the loves that brought
us to our knees
with their disappearance?
only memories remain,
a few words –
and perhaps, a black hole
in the center of a void
where love,
that garment of belonging
awaits,
to cover us with stillness
wreathed in hope.

Dream Enduring

I dreamed I went
to heaven,
a simple space
ageless and empty
nothing to change
nothing to satisfy the
trace of an insatiable longing.

I entered timidly,
one endless dream enduring,
into a peace and safety
that left no doubt
heaven is arrival
not departure.

death is unadorned reality
no language to fill up the event
no images to cleanse the vision.
this place seems to be a hope
a union
a communion,

blurred, yet all one
infinite whole
marked by a significant
and surprise light
far in the distance,
moving slowly, bringing
a warm shield of air to hold

every thought,
every twinge of feeling
in a dream, true and abiding,
all emptiness charged with
a darkness of love
so deep,
so silent,
so clear,
nothing mattered but letting go
and falling into
the dream enduring love.

Exit

truth is fugitive.
it comes with swift disclosure
and disappears into a
distant mirage.

I sit and wonder
about the bigger events in life.
children
the passions of love
marriage in all its
tribal colors
the births and rebirths
that clutter the days
with unnoticed regularity.

I sort out the old baggage
of memories
and rummage through
discarded visions
to attempt an impression

that will hold a smidge
of truth.

when I relax
and take comfort
in all the realities
I hold as truth,
around the corner
vague yet undisguised
comes the great truth.
death, proud and amorous
and demanding attention,
how to give attention
to so morbid an adventure.

I must strip it bare,
pull away all the language
of disappearance,
put on a pair of glasses,
never used,
the final specs that do not
ask me to see anything
but the last exit sign,
in the distance,

a murky neon entrance
into a dark hole beyond
any truth I have ever met.

that last emptiness
blinking its fading light
in my face calls me
to stand still,
put down the armor
and the weapons,
and those pleasing and
acceptable illusions that
have dressed my mind for
eight decades.

how does one let go?
push the release button
or attempt one more
pillaging in and around
some old ideas,
even a slight unnoticeable
threat of discreet

contrivance or maybe
one last avoidance
before the curtain falls?
no applause for such
an unknowable truth.

When death asks:
"who are you?"
I will answer:
"yours"

Death will open wide
and welcome me to
paradise
the pure eternal freedom
that covers all my fears and
empties me of endless
longing.

Into that final gate
I shall enter.

And in that house,
I shall dwell.

Where there shall be no
cloud nor sun.

No darkness nor dazzling,
but one equal light

No noise nor silence,
but one equal music.

No fears nor hopes,
but one equal possession.

No foes nor friends,
but one equal communion,
and identity.

No ends nor beginning,
but one equal eternity.

- John Donne, *from Sermon XV*